CATS SET VI

RAGDOLL CATS

Jill C. Wheeler
ABDO Publishing Company

visit us at
www.abdopublishing.com

Published by ABDO Publishing Company, PO Box 398166, Minneapolis, MN 55439.
Copyright © 2012 by Abdo Consulting Group, Inc. International copyrights reserved
in all countries. No part of this book may be reproduced in any form without written
permission from the publisher. The Checkerboard Library™ is a trademark and logo of
ABDO Publishing Company.

Printed in the United States of America, North Mankato, Minnesota.
102011
012012

 PRINTED ON RECYCLED PAPER

Cover Photo: Photo by Helmi Flick
Interior Photos: Alamy p. 17; Animal Photography pp. 9, 19; Getty Images pp. 10–11;
    Photos by Helmi Flick pp. 5, 7, 11, 13, 21; Peter Arnold p. 15

Editors: Megan M. Gunderson, BreAnn Rumsch
Art Direction: Neil Klinepier

Library of Congress Cataloging-in-Publication Data

Wheeler, Jill C., 1964-
  Ragdoll cats / Jill C. Wheeler.
      p. cm. -- (Cats)
  Includes index.
  ISBN 978-1-61783-243-7
  1. Ragdoll cat--Juvenile literature. I. Title.
SF449.R34W44 2012
636.8'3--dc23
                                    2011026462

CONTENTS

LIONS, TIGERS, AND CATS

Scientists believe humans first tamed wildcats about 3,500 years ago in Egypt. Cats have been living with humans ever since. Today, **domestic** cats are a part of one in three US households.

All these cats make up one species in the family **Felidae**. Lions, tigers, and other big cats make up the other 36 species in this family.

Ancient farmers first used domestic cats to help keep their grain stores free of rats and mice. Some people still look to cats for their amazing hunting abilities. Many others simply enjoy their company. Ragdoll cats are one **breed** that make excellent pets!

Ragdolls are one of more than 40 different breeds of domestic cats.

Ragdoll Cats

Ragdoll cats are hybrids. This means they did not develop on their own in nature. Rather, a person created the ragdoll **breed**. That person was cat breeder Ann Baker. She lived in Riverside, California.

In the 1960s, Baker became interested in a stray cat she named Josephine. Josephine was a long-haired white cat that lived near Baker's home. Baker created ragdoll cats by selectively breeding Josephine's kittens.

These beautiful cats had a special quality. They tended to go limp in one's arms when picked up! Baker called the new breed "ragdoll" for this reason.

Baker founded the International Ragdoll Cat Association, or IRCA. This group is a breeding registry. Today, multiple cat registries recognize the ragdoll **breed**. These include the **Cat Fanciers' Association (CFA)**.

The Ragdoll Society formed in 1975 to promote the breed. The name was later changed to the Ragdoll Fanciers' Club.

QUALITIES

The ragdoll's sweet, friendly temperament is a big reason this **breed** is so popular. Ragdolls enjoy being with people and are good with children. They tend to follow their humans around the house. Ragdolls also get along well with other pets, including dogs.

People seeking a quiet cat may want to consider a ragdoll. The breed does not make much noise. However, they will let their owners know when they are hungry!

Mellow ragdolls spend most of their time at floor level. They won't jump unless it's to snuggle up on a lap or take a nap on an owner's bed.

Ragdolls are laid-back but also very social. These curious, people-loving felines may even greet guests at the door.

Ragdoll cats are extremely popular. As of 2010, they were the CFA's fourth most popular breed!

Ragdoll owners sometimes compare their cats to dogs. Like dogs, some ragdolls have been taught to play fetch or come when called.

COAT AND COLOR

Ragdoll cats have medium-long coats and large, bushy tails. They feature longer fur around their necks and on their hindquarters.

Plush ragdolls are a pointed **breed**. This means they have dark markings on their faces, ears, legs, and tails. These points can be seal, blue, chocolate, or lilac. Large, oval blue eyes contrast these markings.

Ragdoll breeders recognize van, **bicolored**, colorpoint, and mitted color patterns. Van ragdolls are mostly white. Their color shows only on their ears, tail, and face.

Bicolored ragdolls have white undersides with dark shading in a saddle shape on their backs. They also have a white inverted *V* between their eyes.

Colorpoint ragdolls have dark points with a contrasting, lighter body color. Mitted ragdolls are similar to colorpoints. But they have all-white paws. Their chins and stomachs are also white.

Bicolored coat pattern

Colorpoint coat pattern

SIZE

Ragdoll cats are among the larger cat **breeds**. They are long and solid, with muscular bodies, broad chests, and large hindquarters.

Mature male ragdolls usually weigh between 15 and 20 pounds (7 and 9 kg). Female ragdolls are slightly smaller. Their weight averages from 10 to 15 pounds (4.5 to 7 kg).

All this weight is held up on medium-length legs that end with large, round paws. The ragdoll also has a heavy, strong neck and a wedge-shaped head. Its **muzzle** is rounded, and its medium-sized ears have rounded tips.

These gentle giants are slow to mature. Ragdolls may not reach their final weight until they are about four years old.

Despite their larger size, ragdolls have an elegant look.

CARE

Ragdolls do **shed**, but not excessively. And their silky hair rarely **mats**. Yet, this **breed** still requires grooming two to three times per week. Some ragdolls even enjoy being groomed daily!

Use a steel comb to remove dead hair and undo any tangles. Tangles are most common under the cat's armpits.

Don't forget to trim your cat's claws as needed. This will help prevent damage to furniture and carpet. It is also a good idea to brush your cat's teeth regularly.

Like other breeds, ragdoll cats need regular visits to the veterinarian. There, they will get health checkups and **vaccines**.

If you are not going to **breed** your ragdoll, have it **spayed** or **neutered**. This will help avoid future behavior problems and unwanted kittens.

Gentle ragdoll cats are less likely than other pets to fight back if attacked. So they are safest kept indoors. However, some ragdolls do enjoy going for walks on a leash.

Begin grooming your ragdoll when it is a kitten. This will make it more cooperative during this activity as an adult.

FEEDING

Due to their growth pattern, ragdolls have some special feeding requirements. As you know, these cats take a long time to mature. However, they also have growth spurts. During these times, ragdolls can gain two pounds (1 kg) per month!

Some pet owners may worry about not feeding their cat enough during growth spurts. This can be avoided by allowing the cat to eat whenever it is hungry. Dry cat food can be left out for several hours without spoiling. Water should always be available, too.

All cats are meat eaters, so your ragdoll's food should include meat or other protein. Many types of cat food are available at the pet store. These include dry, moist, and semimoist. Just be sure to choose a high-quality food that is labeled as "complete and balanced."

For your ragdoll kitten's first year, it will need extra protein. Aim for a diet with 30 to 40 percent. A mature ragdoll's diet requires less protein.

Free feeding is often the best way to make sure your growing ragdoll kitten gets enough to eat!

KITTENS

Many female ragdolls can become mothers by 12 months of age. They are **pregnant** for about 65 days. Mother ragdolls can have up to three **litters** per year. Each litter will contain an average of four kittens.

Ragdoll kittens are born nearly all white. As they get older, their fur begins to change color. The points turn the darkest because they are the coolest areas on the kitten's body.

At first, the kittens cannot see or hear. Their senses begin to function in about seven to ten days. Soon, the kittens begin to explore.

By this time, the kittens should be handled by people regularly. This will help them grow used to grooming and being held.

You will have to wait until your kitten is between 12 and 16 weeks old to take it home.

At around 12 weeks old, kittens may receive their first **vaccines**. They should also know how to use a **litter box**. These developments help prepare them for life as pets.

BUYING A KITTEN

Have you decided a ragdoll cat is the perfect **breed** for your family? When buying a ragdoll, it is important to work with a trustworthy breeder. The exact cost will depend on the kitten's **pedigree**.

When it's time to choose your kitten, look for signs of good health. These include clear eyes as well as clean fur and ears.

At home, proper care will help your kitten grow into a happy, healthy cat. Show it where the **litter box** is. And introduce it to new people and surroundings often.

Ragdoll kittens are playful and inventive. They will turn almost any object into a toy. Just avoid toys with small parts that could be swallowed or choked on. With lots of love and attention, your cuddly cat should live 12 to 15 years or more.

A list of reputable ragdoll cat breeders is available on the CFA Web site.

GLOSSARY

bicolored - having two colors.

breed - a group of animals sharing the same ancestors and appearance. A breeder is a person who raises animals. Raising animals is often called breeding them.

Cat Fanciers' Association (CFA) - a group that sets the standards for judging all breeds of cats.

domestic - tame, especially relating to animals.

Felidae (FEHL-uh-dee) - the scientific Latin name for the cat family. Members of this family are called felids. They include lions, tigers, leopards, jaguars, cougars, wildcats, lynx, cheetahs, and domestic cats.

litter - all of the kittens born at one time to a mother cat.

litter box - a box filled with cat litter, which is similar to sand. Cats use litter boxes to bury their waste.

mat - to form into a tangled mass.

muzzle - an animal's nose and jaws.

neuter (NOO-tuhr) - to remove a male animal's reproductive glands.

pedigree - a record of an animal's ancestors.

pregnant - having one or more babies growing within the body.

shed - to cast off hair, feathers, skin, or other coverings or parts by a natural process.

spay - to remove a female animal's reproductive organs.

vaccine (vak-SEEN) - a shot given to prevent illness or disease.

WEB SITES

To learn more about ragdoll cats, visit ABDO Publishing Company online. Web sites about ragdoll cats are featured on our Book Links page. These links are routinely monitored and updated to provide the most current information available.

www.abdopublishing.com

INDEX